MANDALA
WISDOM
SERIES

Transcendence

FINDING PEACE AT THE
END OF LIFE

J. Phillip Jones

MANDALA
San Rafael, California

TABLE

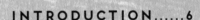

OF CONTENTS

INTRODUCTION

Anthony Jamison was not a religious man; he belonged to no church or denomination and had no inclination to join one. The last day of his life, a Friday afternoon, I pulled into Tony's driveway as he waved at me through the window. We had recently become friends and enjoyed each other's company. About half an hour into our conversation, Tony stopped abruptly, looked out the window, and a few minutes later quit breathing.

Tony had come into our hospice program with some hesitation and a lot of anxiety. An unexpected diagnosis six months earlier had forced him to retire from a job that he loved and "get his affairs in order," as the doctor had suggested. He was shocked and saddened.

As he searched for a way to come to terms with his life and death, Tony noted that he liked the writings of Gandhi. Near the end of his life, during our regular Friday visits, he asked me to read the Mahatma's teachings and discuss them with him. During the last moments of his life, I held Tony's hand and sang the sacred mantras used by his favorite sage, Mahatma Gandhi. In the end, this is where he found his inner peace.

In my thirteen years as a hospice spiritual counselor, I witnessed many ways that people of different faiths and philosophies made peace with life and death before passing. For some it was religion, for many a personal spiritual path; others sang their sacred prayers or chanted their holy mantras. Some found their peace in remembering a beautiful sunset experience, the sound of the ocean, or the awe of a starry night.

Gaining this final peace was fundamentally about that specific person and their special relationship to something deeper and greater than themselves. Making such a connection gave them the strength, wisdom, and courage to cross the final threshold. Nearing the end of life, finding an inner place of spirit, they experienced a state of transcendent peace.

Life is precious and extremely fragile. From one moment to the next, we have no guarantee that we will remain healthy or safe.

When our life or the life of a loved one is threatened, we may reflect: Who am I? What was this life? What is death? Is there life beyond the demise of my body? How can I find the way to inner peace amidst this confusion and chaos?

Philosophers and prophets have examined these questions over the ages. The Vedic sages of India believe that death is feared only when left hidden in the shadows of our ignorance. Death—when exposed to the light of wisdom—can be understood, even embraced, in the service of peace, maturity, and enlightenment.

Transcendence draws on the wisdom of Vedic teachers but resonates with the great teachers and elders of all faiths. A common theme among these teachings is to see birth and death as doorways into and out of the great journey of life. In this way, life is seen as an adventure, a pilgrimage with joys, trials, and tribulations but certainly with a greater purpose writ large behind the changing scenes.

The purpose of this book is to share with the reader an Eastern perspective on living, dying, and death. I hope that some elements of this approach to a spiritual art of dying may be helpful to all readers, especially those who are going through their own dying process or who are supporting a family member or friend nearing the end of life.

Is dying sacred? Can it be practiced or learned as an art or science? We know intuitively and by being with dying people that a twofold process often takes place during the end-of-life experience: first, letting go of the world, family, friends, hopes, and dreams, and second, embracing something infinite within ourselves (soul, essence) and greater than ourselves (Ultimate Reality, God).

The dying process tends to initiate a natural detachment from the finite and a movement toward the Infinite. We think of the Buddha's teachings on detaching from the finite: "Detachment is the doorway to release from suffering." And we think of Jesus's teachings on attachment to the Infinite: "Love the Lord, thy God, with all thy heart, mind, soul, and might."

In the Vedic tradition of India, these two great teachings come together as echoed in this famous passage from the Upanishads:

> Lead us from the unreal to the Real
> Lead us from darkness unto Light
> Lead us from death to Immortality.

There is a way to inner peace laid out in the wisdom teachings of India that works with the natural process of dying, moving us from a preoccupation with the declining body-mind to a focus on the unassailable and immortal spirit.

Significantly, the art of dying is important for each of us at any stage of life. We are all on a pilgrimage of life that culminates in the final rite of passage—death. The time of this final rite is unknown to us or any other human being. Thus we are wise to learn the sacred art of dying, to find the peace that comes with this wisdom, and to live fearlessly in the blessings of each precious day of life.

It is never too late to shine the light of wisdom on our human mortality and our divine immortality. Indeed, during the nearing–death period even more accessible and abundant grace is available to realize the peace, wisdom, and love that can make our Great Transition a powerful rite of passage.

Namaste,

Phillip Jones
Sonoma, California

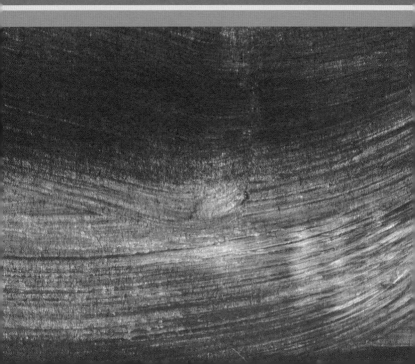

CHAPTER 1

THE LAST RITE
OF PASSAGE

The Last Rite

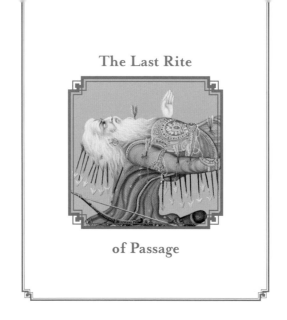

of Passage

> "For the soul there is neither birth nor death. Nor having been will it ever cease to be. The soul is unborn, primeval, ever-existing, and undying. When the body dies, the immortal soul lives on."

—Bhagavad Gita 2.20

A SPIRITUAL OPPORTUNITY

Jacob lay dying at the age of seventy-one. He had finally come to peace with himself after a difficult life. Jacob was living in one room of a little cottage surrounded by the Nature that he loved. He had already given away most of his prized possessions. Jacob even gave his ex-wife his last $2,000 as a farewell present. Every day friends and neighbors came by, first to console him in his dying days, but later to receive his blessings. I had heard him on more than one occasion give comfort and counsel to a friend in need. Jacob had gotten past the crisis of dying and come to see it for what it is: the body's end and the soul's *liberation. He once told me that his own spiritual teacher had died in Jacob's arms with a smile on his face. In that moment, Jacob decided to live his life in such a way that he would be able to die in peace when his time came. Now, he looked at me with the eyes of one who has dropped all of the masks of ego and can only speak truth. "I've never been happier in my life," he said. "In the end, it's all about love." Jacob radiated infinite love, having let go of all attachments to finite things. And this freedom made him attractive to all who saw him. Jacob created a peaceful atmosphere in his little room with sacred music and scents. He continued to read a variety of spiritual books. And we enjoyed conversations on transcendental matters up until the last days of his life. When Jacob first came into hospice, he posed questions to me: "Who am I really?" "What is God?" Near the end, Jacob was answering those questions from his own inner realizations. His dying was noble and powerful, giving showers of blessings to those who came near. Jacob's death was not a tragedy but a testament to the incredible spiritual opportunity of dying in wisdom, love, and grace.*

THE QUESTIONS OF A DYING PERSON

I have sat at the bedsides of hundreds of men and women in the days and months before their deaths. Most people who know they are dying begin to reflect on life. They ponder: Who am I? What was my life all about? Is there a life after death? Who or what is God? Will I be judged for my deeds? Am I a good person? Does anyone truly love or care for me now that I'm dying?

The Vedic sages of India have contemplated these questions for thousands of years through the study of divinely revealed wisdom texts and in states of deep meditation. In this book, we will examine the Vedic perspective on these and other questions that are important to all of us. They become especially important if we are facing death.

The answer to the first question—"Who am I?"—is at the heart of the Vedic wisdom teachings. Without understanding the nature of our self, it becomes difficult to understand almost anything related to our existence. The sages say that our true nature is immortal spirit, but we are caught up in the mistake of thinking that we are only a body and a mind.

An example is given to illustrate the immensity of this mistake. A princess is traveling through the desert alone. She has an accident that induces amnesia. She forgets who she is. The young woman wanders into a nearby town. She eventually must get a job in order to survive. She becomes a fruit vendor at the local marketplace. The woman lives a difficult life for years in this little town, not knowing her real identity. One day her amnesia goes away, and she remembers who she is. "I'm the king's daughter!" she shouts out loud. Although the local people think that she has lost her mind, she immediately leaves the town, travels back to her home at the palace, and takes up the life of royalty again. All of her lesser problems are solved by remembering her true identity.

In our state of forgetfulness, we suffer through the ups and downs of human life, not knowing that we are immortal beings on a journey through the material universe. Whenever and wherever we can grasp the lesson of the soul, our life becomes

sublime. Even if our physical body is threatened with extinction, realizing that we are soul can bring us to a state of fearlessness and joy. If indeed we are dying, that dying can become a noble departure—a powerful rite of passage from this earth school to our next destination. It is never too early and never too late to learn the lesson of the soul's immortality.

EVERY BODY DIES, BUT NO ONE DIES

It is a natural part of life that our journey in a material body comes to an end. It is indeed a human tragedy for those left behind, who will miss the physical presence of their loved one. But dying is not a tragedy for those who are aware of what it really is.

Eastern religions have always been clear on the difference between a person's true identity and their physical or mental coverings. The body is a wonderful gift, but it is not who we are. It is sacred, in that it provides a home or temple for the spirit. We certainly want to take care of our body, nurturing it in every way. However, too much attachment to the body leads to confusion, pain, and suffering. For example, if I have a nice car and someone smashes the fender in a parking lot, I may become angry and agitated. I will suffer to the extent of my attachment to that vehicle. In the well-known Indian scripture the Bhagavad Gita, Lord Krishna counsels his friend Arjuna to find security in the spirit rather than in the fallible bodily vehicle. Krishna says: "Never was there a time when I did not exist, nor you, nor all these warriors. Nor in the future shall any of us cease to be." What is that "I" which has always existed? It is certainly not the body, which anyone can see is temporary. What continues to exist when the body stops functioning? What never dies is the immortal self, which the Vedas call the atma, or soul. In other words, every body dies, but no one dies. I ask that we consider what is really dying. According to the Vedic wisdom, our body may be dying, but we, the soul, are not. We are immortal.

GOODNESS, PERFECTION, AND IMMORTALITY

A common question asked by people nearing death is, "Am I a good person?" There are various philosophical schools of thought that debate whether humans are inherently good or bad. The Vedic sages clearly state that all beings are good and perfect in their true nature. The ancient scripture Isa Upanishad says: "From the All Perfect come perfect emanations; all beings come from the Perfect Being and return to perfection in the end."

One of the most important messages of the Vedic teachings is this: Although we inhabit mortal frames that eventually decline and pass away, our inherent nature is always good, perfect, and immortal because of its good, perfect, and immortal Source. If we all come from God, or the Divine Source, then we share in the goodness and perfection of that Source. This is an important meditation during life, but it becomes especially important as death draws near and our body deteriorates. We may soberly look to the moment when our body ceases to work, yet we can joyfully look to the same moment, when the perfection of our spirit is glimpsed.

The beauty of the Vedic teachings on dying is this: If we are able to simply remember who we are and the Source from which we come, we can attain the home of our soul at the time of death.

As we wrap up our earthly affairs, reconcile with family and friends, and express regrets for actions wrongly taken, we become free to reflect on our true nature. The sages say that we are good because we come from the all-good. We are loved because we come from the source of love.

If we are approaching death, we can let go of our earthly life of joys and sorrows, victories and mistakes. We may now look inside at our perfect, good, and immortal soul and, with the eyes of the soul, meditate on the Supreme Soul. Filling the mind and heart with thoughts of the Supreme, especially at the moment of death, is the ancient method used by the sages of India to pass from this world into perfection.

LOSING THE WORLD, GAINING IMMORTALITY

Realization of the immortal self is not always easy, even with the urgency of our physical decline. The dying process appears to be a paradox. We lose many of the things that have defined our life: health, beauty, strength, influence, and the ability to travel and enjoy our wealth. Yet we have an opportunity to gain the greatest treasure of all: our true immortal identity.

According to the Vedic sages, this paradox arises because of the common human confusion over our true identity. Are we an ego that continually has to defend its possessions, wealth, family, image, status, and the like? Or are we a soul that is defined by its intrinsic worth as immortal, wise, and joyful? It does not take much wisdom to realize that the latter option is preferable. Yet our culture promotes the former conception of self, blinded as it is by a fascination with the fleeting promises of material life.

During the dying process, the ego begins to weaken because all of its supports (good health, position, possessions) begin to lose their importance. Because of our conditioning, especially if we live in a materialistic culture, we feel we are losing much of who we are. We suffer emotionally because of this misidentification. It is not unusual that a dying person begins to wonder if they are a person anymore: Do I have value? What am I worth, since I'm losing all of the things that have defined me?

The Vedic tradition, however, affirms that our worth does not diminish in the least with any harm to the body or mind.

As Krishna tells Arjuna in the Bhagavad Gita, "The soul cannot be pierced by weapons, burned by fire, wet by water, or withered by the wind." If a $20 bill is crumpled and worn out, is it any less valuable than a brand-new $20 bill? No, the value is precisely the same. Similarly our true value is not diminished in any way by the loss or decline of the props of the ego.

The dying process, with its numerous losses, can become a powerful opportunity to let go of the ego's hold on our identity and finally discover our true nature as spirit. The ego's lifelong striving to defend itself from all attacks on its value is over. We can relax into spirit. We can find refuge, strength, and empowerment in our identity as immortal soul.

PREPARING FOR THE NEARING-DEATH TIME

Death is a part of life for all of us. But for someone who has received a terminal diagnosis, it immediately becomes the most dominant part of life. The nearing death experience is unique for every one of us, but thoughtful societies throughout history have seen death not just as a tragic end to a unique individual life, but as one of life's Great Transitions, or rites of passage. Seen in this light, preparation for death becomes more than tearful goodbyes and waiting to expire. Historically, in most of the great faith traditions, the person who was approaching death was prepared by family, friends, and clergy for this great passage.

Just as a young girl or boy was prepared for the transition to adulthood, or a bride was prepared to be married, so a friend or family member was prepared for death. Sacred texts such as the Tibetan Book of the Dead, the Christian Ars Moriendi, and the Vedic Bhagavad Gita gave guidance to the candidates for the passage from earthly life. These texts recognize the continuance of the soul or life force beyond the expiration of the physical body.

The nearing-death period may be said to begin once a terminal prognosis has been given and all lifesaving techniques have been exhausted. An important part of the nearing-death experience is the quality of living prior to death. A person's quality of life during the nearing-death period can be considered in two ways:

Is the person able to live the day-to-day experience of earthly life with gratitude?

Is the person able to progress in his or her preparation for the next world?

This period can be a time of existential suffering or tremendous growth, depending on the answers to these two questions. Unfortunately, for some people looking at a terminal diagnosis, the only question becomes, "How long do I have to wait to die?" They are not able to see any reason to go on living when death looms near.

HOPING TO LIVE, ACCEPTING OUR DYING

First, let us consider the day-to-day experience of earthly life when our days have been numbered by a doctor or other medical professional. If indeed we have tried all means to return to health and nothing has worked, we have a decision to make: Am I to accept that I'm really dying, or should I hope for a miracle? In a very real sense, we can do both.

Vedic wisdom says that the length of our life is predetermined by our purpose in this life and our karma from past lives. Our days are numbered by Destiny and thus out of our—or any other human being's—hands. This doesn't mean that we should hesitate to use all means at our disposal to return to health. But neither the greatest doctor nor the greatest medicine can save us if our time has arrived. As the Vedic saying goes: "If God wants to save us, nothing can kill us; and if God wants to take us, nothing can save us."

So where does this leave us? It leaves us with the option to accept our coming death with a hope that it may not be our time. Perhaps it is our destined time to die; or perhaps our life's purpose is not complete, and an unexpected healing will occur so we can complete it. Either way, it is out of our hands. Realizing this, we can relax and fully experience each moment of our life, prepared to live out all of our days and be ready to depart if that is our current destiny. Letting go of the pressure to either fight for our life or to accept our dying is a great relief. In this way, another paradox regarding living and dying may be resolved.

LIVING FULLY IN THE PRESENT MOMENT

With the pressure of fighting or letting go diminished, we now have the opportunity to simply live in the present moment, the present day of life. People in recovery talk about living "one day at a time." This is good advice for all of us, especially if we feel we are in that netherworld between life and death. This is a time that for many can be the least burdensome time of their lives. The pressures of living are coming to an end. Relatives and friends often step up to reconcile old differences or to take over worldly responsibilities. We have been given some precious time to reflect on our life, to integrate the lessons of our life, and to grow in spirit through that integration. Whether we recover or die, this is a potentially powerful time of life and a significant transition: If we recover, our life will never be the same; if we die, our life will never be the same. Proper introspection during this time can bring immense rewards in this life and the next.

THE SOUL EVOLVES UNTIL THE LAST MOMENT OF LIFE

The second measure of our quality of life during this time relates not to the day-to-day life of peaceful existence, but to the soul's continued schooling and growth. The second reason then to go on living when we are no longer "productive" is clear in the Vedic texts: The soul continues to evolve, grow, and deepen its connection to God in all stages of life, particularly in this special period of time. Dr. Kathleen Singh's research in her excellent book *The Grace in Dying* records numerous cases of people nearing death who unexpectedly make rapid spiritual progress. What she calls "surrender of the ego and transcendence into a union with Spirit" has been observed in many dying people. In other words, as physical, mental, and social "productivity" declines, the potential for soul growth increases exponentially. If our physical pain and symptoms can be mostly brought under control, and our earthly business and family affairs can be wrapped up, we may find ourselves poised on the brink of a potential spiritual evolution.

HOW SHALL WE DIE?

Accepting that the soul is able to grow and evolve up until the passage called death, we have a choice on how to spend the last days and months of our lives. Knowing that the dying

phase of life is the last rite of passage allows us to plan and live this life stage as successfully as we have transited other stages: adolescence, marriage or partnership, midlife, retirement, and perhaps even sagehood. The dying phase of life can be considered the culmination of our sage years. Ideally, we have learned as students, produced as adults, mentored others in our wisdom years, and moved toward universal love in our sage years.

Even if we have not fully achieved the goals of our various life stages, now we are preparing to pass on to a place of higher wisdom and love. Since this last phase of life is the most powerful stage and appears to be a time of tremendous grace, we can prepare for a successful transition even if we have not lived a long life or do not feel complete in the earlier stages.

During the dying phase of life, the possibility of existential suffering exists as we lose physical, mental, and social abilities. Many dying people lament that they continue to lose things week after week—their job, their mobility, their social life, their hearing, their ability to read, and ultimately their life. Even with all of the best pain medications, still these losses may lead to a psychological or existential pain that can only be addressed by spiritual means.

One way to approach this dying phase of life is as a rite of passage. The vision quest, pilgrimage, or rite of passage in great cultures, including the Vedic culture, is a time when the quester and his or her supporters accept the challenge of a life crisis as an opportunity for growth, as opposed to a time of stress and suffering. In all of our life passages, we have this same choice: Will adolescence, midlife, retirement, or dying be a time of failure and stress or a time of quantum growth to embrace the next natural phase of life?

A Gallup poll in 1997 found four spiritual concerns high on the list of people who were in the stage of dying:

Not being reconciled with others—56%
Not being forgiven by God—56%
Dying when feeling cut off from God or a
    Higher Power—51%
Fear of the possibility of emotional/spiritual
    suffering after death—51%

These fears and others may lead to a type of suffering that is not treatable by pain medication. In recent years, advances in medical pain relief have been impressive. Especially in the hospice setting, with its focus on comfort care versus cure, we see that a large percentage of hospice patients find relief from all or most physical pain. Dame Cicely Saunders, founder of the modern hospice movement, determined that, in addition to treating physical pain, end-of-life care must consider total suffering (which includes mental, emotional, and spiritual pain).

When a person is faced with a terminal illness, they often look back with regret at an incomplete or unsatisfying life, or look forward with fear to an uncertain future. Thus, existential or spiritual suffering may include one or more of the following concerns: having no reconciliation with family or friends; experiencing guilt over bad choices made or dreams unfulfilled; not being prepared for death; feeling abandoned by people and by God in the present; having fear of dying and judgment by God in the future; and being confused about the meaning of life and the cause of suffering.

Rather than approaching each of the above problems individually, a comprehensive way to address all these types of fear and suffering is to change the lens through which we view the dying stage of life itself. As shown in the chart below, we can consider two ways to view death and two ways to die. We may view death as an unknowable, frightening phenomenon in which we ultimately lose everything of value. Or we can view death as a rite of passage. We may then approach death in one of two ways: unprepared, in denial, and vulnerable to suffering, or consciously prepared to "ride the tiger of fate" through our final life passage.

Dying Unconsciously (Existential suffering)	Dying Consciously (As a rite of passage)
Not hungry, not eating	Reduced eating or fasting
Isolation/loneliness	Isolation/aloneness
Losing former identity	Letting go of former identity
Focused on the body and mind	Focused on the immortal soul
Disconnected from / rejected by the world	Letting go of the material world
Reflecting on one's life (judging)	Reflecting on one's life (accepting)
Resisting guidance, counsel	Seeking a vision, guidance, and counsel
Uncertain about the future (fearful)	Uncertain about the future (excited)
Fearing death	Accepting of physical and ego death
Punished by a judging God or an impersonal Universe	Child of a loving God and a friendly Universe

AN EASY CHOICE: CONSCIOUS DYING

The Vedic wisdom teachings make this choice easy. The Vedas declare: We are immortal souls beyond birth and death; this life is a short journey in a temporary world with the opportunity for spiritual growth; and God is all-loving and welcomes all souls back to the spiritual world when their "schooling" is complete. Thus, we may let go of viewing death as a tragedy and instead choose the noble path of conscious dying, asking our spiritual friends and loved ones to support us in this last rite of passage.

Jane was a sixty-year-old medical professional who was dying. She had taken up Eastern spiritual practices late in life and told her hospice nurse that she wanted to minimize any numbing pain medication and maximize her ability to be conscious through the dying process. She told me with a big grin on her face that she was very excited to experience dying and death. Jane held true to her desire and dealt with a little more pain than some of us would want, but died on her own terms. She said shortly before her death that she was prepared for the ride of her life.

Gloria was an older woman who stopped eating by her own choice at a certain point in her dying process. Her relatives were quite concerned and attempted to persuade her to start eating again. But she said she had gotten an inner signal that it was time for her body to shut down. Gloria was a religious Catholic woman. She told me that her spirit was being nourished by her faith and her body just wanted to rest. Gloria gracefully passed into the next world as her spirit slipped away peacefully.

Ben was forty-six years old and dying. He had moved to Hawaii three years before to live out his dream in paradise. Ben was pain-free physically, but he was experiencing serious depression and anxiety. During a conversation with Ben, he related to me that his life had been a failure. "I never amounted to anything," he said. "I never held a good job, never made much money; my life was a failure." I asked Ben to go into more depth about his life. Finally he said, "Well, a lot of people said I was a good listener. They would come to me to talk about things that were going wrong in their lives. They said it made them feel better to know that someone understood and cared about them." I was then able to confidently and honestly assure Ben that his earth journey had been a success: He had learned lessons of kindness and love; he had helped others on their difficult journeys; he had been a friend and confidant. Ben looked amazed and slowly smiled, "I guess you're right, if you put it that way." He visibly relaxed for the first time since I met him. Ben was able to die at peace with himself, knowing that he had grown in the earth school, and had made a difference in others' lives.

These three true-life examples make it clear that our dying phase of life can be successful if we are able to let go of the material way of judging success—money, good jobs, gourmet eating, lack of suffering—and look at life during our Great Transition as a soul evolution, a rite of passage with incredible opportunities for spiritual growth. The chart on page 26 about conscious and unconscious dying can be a useful blueprint to help us take the conscious road through the dying process.

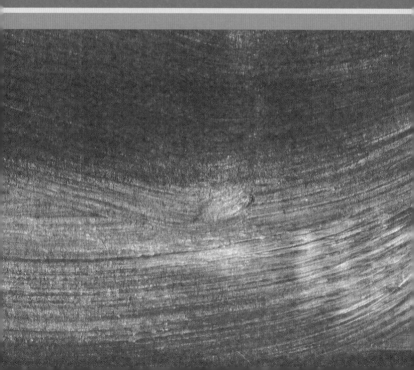

CHAPTER 2

DYING IN HIGHER
CONSCIOUSNESS

Dying in Higher

Consciousness

"Whatever state of being one remembers at
the time of death, that state he will attain
without fail. And one who remembers Me at the
moment of death attains the highest abode."
—Bhagavad Gita 8.5–6

A GOOD DEATH

Traditional Vedic culture describes death as a significant
event, at which time the state of one's consciousness is of
the utmost importance. Prior to the last hundred years, most
people died in their own homes, surrounded by friends, family,
and perhaps a local doctor or priest. Rather than in a hospital,
hooked up to tubes with IV drips and subject to doctors using
electric shocks trying to revive a body that has given out, the most
important end-of-life task of "dying in higher consciousness"
is often better attained at home, with limited drugs, passionate
activity, and whirring machines.

THE KING WHO WAS CURSED TO DIE IN SEVEN DAYS

What, then, is a good death? The Vedic teachings relate the story of an Indian king named Pariksit who was told that he would die in seven days. He immediately left his palace and sat down at a sacred river to fast and hear from great teachers how to prepare for death. It should be noted that King Pariksit was at the height of his material potency. He had a great kingdom and a loving family, and he was well respected by his subjects. Like many people, the king was living in the midst of a good life when death unexpectedly drew near.

The story relates that King Pariksit had been on a forest expedition when he came to a sage's hut. Asking for food and water, the king was ignored by the sage who was absorbed in a state of deep meditation. Misunderstanding the sage's mind, King Pariksit became angry and insulted him by throwing a dead snake around his neck. The sage's meditation was undisturbed by this offense, but the sage's young son happened to arrive on the scene and cursed the king. The boy said, "On the seventh day from today a snake will bite and kill this unqualified king for having insulted my innocent father." When the sage came out of his meditation he was appalled to hear what his son had done, but a curse once spoken could not be undone.

The pious king took this event as his destiny and consequently prepared himself for death. According to the Srimad Bhagavatam, in which this story is told, the king accepted the curse as good news, for it would be the cause of his indifference toward worldly things. He welcomed the forewarning that gave him seven days to prepare for his last rite of passage.

Pariksit immediately gave up his position as king, turned over the kingdom to his eldest son, said goodbye to his family and friends, and went straight to the bank of the sacred river Ganges to fast and hear spiritual teachings until his death in seven days. The story relates that King Pariksit freed himself from all kinds of material attachments and accepted the vows of a sage. Since the king would not be able to go through the natural stages of life—student, householder, retiree, and sage—he immediately fixed his mind in the consciousness of a sage in the last stage of life.

THE KING'S SUPPORTERS GATHER IN A SACRED PLACE

News of King Pariksit's decision spread throughout the land, and many great thinkers, sages, and pilgrims came to support the king in his Great Transition. Indeed, it is said that sages from other planets in the universe also came to this unusual gathering. These sages added to the purified atmosphere of the sacred place chosen by the king to be most favorable for his passing.

The king spoke to the sages: "Oh great sages, please accept me as a soul prepared to meet God. I have taken the Lord into my heart. Let the snake bite me at once. I only desire that all of you continue to speak to me of the glories of the Supreme."

In that sacred place, surrounded by spiritually mature people, the king became completely free from all fear of death. He sat down in meditation on a straw mat facing north.

The king then asked the sages to instruct him on what specifically a person should do at the time of death. At that moment, a young sage arrived whose countenance surpassed all others. All of the sages noticed this and offered the enlightened youth a seat directly in front of the king. This teacher, known as Sukadeva, sat with the king for the next seven days, speaking of the immortal soul and the glories of God, instructing him how to prepare to leave this world in perfect consciousness. At the end of one week, Pariksit left the earth planet in full consciousness while chanting sacred names and was liberated to the transcendental realm.

LESSONS FOR DEPARTING WELL: ACHIEVING A GOOD DEATH

The story of King Pariksit is very insightful as to how one with a short amount of time to live can prepare for a successful departure from this world. Often our hospice patients receive a terminal diagnosis of a few weeks. This is generally very frightening to the patient as well as his or her family members. It seems cruel, unfair, and tragic. And, on a human level, it is. However, the king accepted his one-week death notice with intelligence and dignity. He quickly let go of any attachments to status, worldly power, unfinished business, incomplete dreams, and unresolved relationships. He looked at life through a different lens once he knew that he was going to die soon.

With only seven days to live, the king decided to take the radical step of immediately departing for a sacred place to live in sacred time for the week leading up to his death. The Indian culture at that time supported such an extreme choice. Although we live in different times, quickly letting go of the attachment to temporary pleasures, possessions, and power is always a good choice, especially if we know that death is drawing near. In the time nearing death, one is well advised to focus on the next plane while simultaneously letting go of this world.

I have observed many people nearing death who begin to look into the next world, speak with those who have already departed, and generally let go of old baggage for a light journey into the spiritual realm. I remember a grandmother who began to frighten her family members by talking to people who were not there—until a young grandson walked into her bedroom and asked about the bright man in white clothes standing in the corner.

The king also found a suitable spiritual environment—both the sacred environment of the holy river and the social environment of people who were aligned with his desire for a spiritual passing. We also find that some people nowadays intelligently create a spiritual environment in their living space and restrict their visitors to those coming with a positive outlook to support their transition in the way that they choose.

Most importantly, the king did not waste time complaining about his fate but made his needs known to his group of supporters. His spiritual advisor came and taught him the most succinct and practical ways in which he could prepare himself for dying, especially advising that he remember God through chanting the Holy Names. This simple technique is also advised for modern-day nearing-death journeyers, as most all of the world religions have teachings on the power of remembering and singing sacred sound vibrations to prepare the soul for departure.

A GOOD DEATH IN MODERN TIMES

"Mom was pulling up the hair at the top of her head. I think she felt her soul trying to leave through the crown," she said. Rachel had lost her mother to breast cancer recently, and now sat by the bed of her husband who was only days away from dying of prostate cancer. Her husband, Robert, had been a drug abuser earlier in his life but had made a remarkable move toward the spiritual life in recent decades. Robert and Rachel seemed to have an ecumenical approach to religion. I knew that they had Christian friends, a Hawaiian elder with whom they had apprenticed, and that they had recently visited a Buddhist temple. I had been alone with Robert the previous week and experienced an unusual phenomenon. As we sat together in meditation, I experienced myself looking through his eyes at his small room filled with spiritual objects and felt a sense of deep peace. I sensed that our work together was coming to a close and that Robert would make his transition soon.

Robert and I had shared spiritual insights over the five months he had been in hospice. He had traveled the world, experiencing the spiritual flavor of exotic places like Bali and many islands in the South Pacific. He had come to know that Spirit pervades all living beings and thus felt connected to God in a very informal, personal way. But on this day Robert was unresponsive, breathing slowly through his oxygen tube as his wife and a friend kept vigil.

And now Rachel was telling me that her mother's soul had possibly left through her crown chakra. Although I had not spent much time with Rachel, I now knew that I could share with her some suggestions for this critical time. Before leaving, I suggested that Rachel chant sacred songs to her husband to help his passage from this world. She surprised me as she nodded: "Yes, I did that once before when a woman had a heart attack in a parking lot. I was the closest person around. As she lay dying in my arms, all I could think to do was to chant the name of Krishna. Is it OK if I chant Krishna or Govinda to Robert?" I assured her that chanting the names of God would be the perfect thing to do. Robert died peacefully two days later as his wife chanted softly to him.

THE FACE OF GOD YOU SEE AT DEATH

At the moment of death, everyone has an opportunity to see God. We know this from ancient wisdom teachings as well as modern-day reports of near-death experiences. People who "die" according to the reckoning of medical science but later begin to breathe again often report an encounter with a bright light or a soothing voice. Some of the "deceased" witness a divine being who informs them that it is not their destined time to die and that they need to return to complete some unfinished aspect of their life. According to a person's faith, this encounter may be with God, a prophet, or a saint, as described in their particular sacred texts.

The Vedic teachings describe God in three different ways. First, God is known as Brahman, the Great Spirit or impersonal light that pervades the universe. Second, God is the inner teacher known as Paramatma, the silent voice of conscience within us that can give us guidance during our lives. God is also known as Bhagavan, the Supreme Loving Being who awaits our graduation to the next level of development. The Vedas say that God is both personal and impersonal, immanent and transcendent. Thus, these are not three different phenomena, but One Being viewed from different angles of vision. For example, at a great distance we may see a fuzzy light coming from the top of a hill. As we get closer to this light, we see that it is a campfire. And as we get to the site of the campfire, we see the person who created the campfire.

These three "faces of God" described in the Vedic tradition are really different ways of viewing One Ultimate Reality. Which face of God a person may see at death depends on the relationship with divinity one has cultivated during one's life. The Vedas encourage us to cultivate a strong connection to divinity by acknowledging all of these faces of God—God as the Supreme Person, God as the inner voice of wisdom, and God as the all-pervading spirit. However, especially significant for most dying people is the ability to feel a relationship with God the Supreme Person, as they are leaving all of the important relationships of their earthly life.

As we prepare a friend or loved one to make the death transition, we may encourage them to go to the light, listen to their inner divine guidance, and surrender into God's arms. This is some of the best counsel we can give to the departing soul. As they approach the veil that divides this world from the next, most people have some fear, especially due to the uncertainty of what is awaiting them on the other side. We can know with confidence that God is there to escort the souls who are willing to reach out. In fact, there are many reports of people who have reached out to grasp an unseen hand in the last seconds of life.

RELATIVITY AND THE
LESSONS OF LOVE

Life is short, we sense, as a beloved family member faces their last days. On the other hand, a friend once surprised me by solemnly declaring that "life is long." He was in the middle of a major and difficult transition in his life. Such differences in the perception of time explain a lot. Albert Einstein once commented that an hour with the one we love passes like a second, while a few seconds sitting on a hot stove can seem like an eternity. "This," he declared, "summarizes Relativity."

In hospice, we have the honor and privilege of being with people in the intimate, sometimes frightening final phase of their lives. Time during these days is truly relative. Some say, "It's passing so quickly—I just don't have enough time." Others declare, "It's so slow, why can't I die? I'm just waiting to die." Fortunately, for most people who are dying, reconciliation and acceptance are attained before their last breath.

I have learned many lessons journeying with people who are dying. I have especially come to appreciate the preciousness and relative brevity of a human life, and yet the timeless seconds of life in a profound present moment. There always seems to be time, in the present moment, to forgive, to receive, to find peace, to love, even to touch the Absolute. In more than one instance, we have seen a father estranged from a son for decades forgive and embrace that child hours before passing. We have seen spouses in a moment of great release let go of long-held resentments and grudges as the stresses of a long marriage dissolve in the awareness of their underlying love.

What is the moral in these types of stories for the rest of us? Over and again, we hear the message clearly. Numerous times a man or woman near the end has looked into my eyes with eyes that can no longer speak untruth and said these words: "Life is about love. In the end, it's all about love." Those who are conscious in their dying don't obsess on money, or houses, or occupations, or pleasures, or even peace. They speak of love. And those loved ones who sit at the bedside of their beloved for hours and days on end, tending to every physical, emotional, and spiritual need, are the real heroes who continue to impress those of us who assist their vigils of love.

The world religions clearly agree on one thing: Love endures. No scripture or song or doctrine or belief system reflects God or the mystery that sustains us all like the love a bed-bound and helpless person sees in the eyes of their beloved family member, friend, or teacher.

LOVE IS IMMORTAL

And, conversely, what is the unfathomable love that we sometimes see in the eyes of a person who is dying but is full of peace and joy? It is a special type of love, an unselfish and universal love for all beings, for God, and for one's own self, the soul. Finding this divine love at the end can make the dying stage a crown jewel of one's life. If love is the most important phenomenon in this world, what is its place in the next world? According to the Vedic conclusion, love is the central dynamic of all worlds.

Yoga is the name given to the spiritual path of the Vedic sages. Yoga means "yoke," union, relationship. The union sought on the yoga path is the ultimate relationship of the soul with God. There is a yoga of action and a yoga of wisdom. Through selfless actions and knowledge, one may connect or unite with the Divine. But the yoga of love is the deepest and strongest way of connecting with God and all beings.

Even secular people in this world have some intuition that love is so powerful that it transcends even death. The ancient scripture known as Narada's Bhakti-sutra goes a step further and declares that love and the devotion it engenders is the very quintessence of immortality: "Having obtained it, a person becomes perfect, immortal, and peaceful . . . therefore this devotional love alone is to be followed by the seekers of liberation."

OPENING THE DOORWAY TO TRUTH AS DEATH APPROACHES

We have discussed the fears associated with a dying person's unresolved past, uncertain future, and isolated present. Narada declares that love is the doorway to truth and happiness in past, present, and future. What does this mean for our sojourn through the valley of death? It means for the past that the essence of our earth life has not been what we possessed or were able to buy, but the love of soul, others, and God that we have cultivated. And for the future, we can be assured, according to the Vedic sages, that the loving union of all souls with God and with each other is at the heart of the spiritual world.

The culmination of the spiritual path of yoga is the never-ending and always-expanding loving devotion of souls and God. Beyond all actions and all wisdom, love reigns supreme. This is echoed as well in the various world religions. Saint Paul stated it well when he declared that three things abide forever: "Faith, hope, and love . . . but the greatest of these is love."

The Vedic sages have declared that attachment to the "unreal," temporary things of this world is the cause of all suffering. The Buddha made this understanding one of the foundational points of his teachings. In this mortal world, selfishness drives us to reach out for temporary pleasures and possessions, a preoccupation that comes to a crashing halt when death approaches. But the sages also declare that attachment to the Real—love of God, our soul, and all other souls—is the very source of all happiness.

The key, then, to embracing the approach of death is to embrace our life's ending in love. We can feel gratitude for each beautiful sunrise and sunset, each breeze, each fragrant flower, and especially each smiling face of family members and friends who come to support our spiritual journey through the doorway of death. Most of all, we can relax into the loving embrace of Spirit, a Divine Being who awaits our graduation to the next level of wisdom and love.

THE LAST TASKS OF LIFE

In summary, the Vedic tradition counsels us to prepare for our Great Transition in three ways:

(1) Letting go of the world and resolving all karma
(2) Turning to the soul and to God
(3) Making the transition as consciously as possible

Letting go of the world and resolving all karma. We have explored some ways in which people let go of worldly affairs by turning over unfinished business to family and friends, accepting their life regardless of shortcomings, and especially resolving old grudges, resentments, and misunderstanding. A great teacher from India who passed away only a few years ago called one of his close friends to his side as he was nearing death. He asked his spiritual brother to go and find any person whom he had offended in any way by his bold teaching activities, and to beg pardon on his behalf. This teacher was, in fact, acknowledged as a saint by many people. Yet he continued to teach by showing the importance of leaving the world free from lingering karma. Many religious people facing death in India take death's approach as an opportunity to go to friends and enemies alike to apologize for misunderstanding, to give away possessions to those in need, and to give blessings as well.

Turning to the soul and to God. The word *conversion* means to "turn around" or to "turn away from the world and to turn toward Spirit." In the Vedic tradition, conversion is not a one-time only experience of grace or salvation. One's entire life is a pilgrimage of conversion, and the last phase of life is its culmination. As death draws near, we are urged to turn fully to our immortal soul and to God. Through the use of sacred chants and songs, reading scriptures, listening to holy teachers, visiting sacred places like temples, and creating an environment full of sacred sounds, smells, and vision, the person nearing death seeks to move fully into the transitional state between this world and the next.

Making a conscious transition. Vedic wisdom speaks of the importance of a conscious transition from the world, if possible. It is said that the soul or life force of a person leaves the body through one of the subtle openings of the body (known as chakras). A departure though one of the higher chakras is considered auspicious. The dying person is also encouraged to

minimize the use of mind-numbing drugs, if possible. And, most importantly, he or she is advised to pass away in the highest state of consciousness possible by cultivating detachment from earthly life and the body while attaching to the soul and God.

THE MOMENT OF DEATH

According to Vedic teachings, one's consciousness during the last breath of life determines the soul's destination. To breathe our last in a high state of consciousness is therefore very important. Of course, our last thoughts will mainly be determined by the thoughts and deeds of our entire lifetime. We are unlikely to have noble thoughts at the moment of death if we have lived a life of brutality and vice. Through spiritual practice during our life, however, we are able to depart the world in high consciousness. In modern times, Mahatma Gandhi's departure exemplified this concept. When Gandhi was shot, the last word from his mouth was a name of God ("Rama"). Gandhi was raised by his grandmother to always meditate on God's name as a spiritual practice, and he successfully left the world with God's name on his lips.

King Pariksit's death in ancient times and Gandhi's death in the twentieth century are reminders to us that anyone can successfully transit death by meditating on divine names at the end of life. The scriptures teach that the names of God are unlimited and all-powerful. Not only the Vedic texts but also many other scriptures recommend chanting or meditating on sacred sound vibrations as one departs the world. This is the last and most important task for the dying person, according to ancient and modern Vedic teachers.

If you believe that you or a loved one is approaching death, consider these last tasks to be time-tested ways to prepare for a good dying process and a powerful and successful departure. If you are not familiar with sacred chants, see appendix A for Vedic mantras that may be used as a spiritual practice as death draws near.

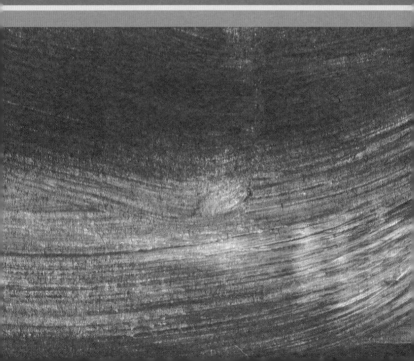

CHAPTER 3

SOULS AND
THEIR DESTINATIONS

Souls and

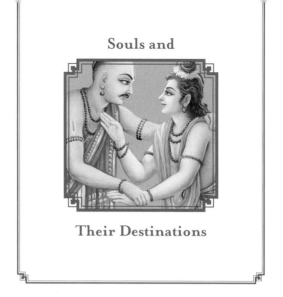

Their Destinations

"A man acts according to the desires to which he clings. After death he goes to the next world bearing in mind the subtle impressions of his deeds; and after reaping there the harvest of his deeds, he returns again to this world of action. Thus, he who has desires is subject to rebirth."

—Brihadaranyaka Upanishad 4.4.5–6

"From the highest planet to the lowest, all are places where birth and death occur. But one who comes to My abode never takes birth again."

—Bhagavad Gita 8.16

A UNIVERSE BASED ON LOVE

Vedic cosmology tells of two realms of existence: a spiritual realm and a "reflected" material counterpart. In the Upanishads and the Bhagavad Gita, the material realm is described metaphorically as "a great banyan tree with its roots upward and its branches down." Where have we seen such a tree? Reflected in the water of a pond. The real tree is on the bank of the pond; the reflected tree with roots upward and branches down is an inverted version of the real tree. The Vedic sages realized in their meditation that the world of matter, consisting of the entire material universe, is like such an inverted tree and not the real world of the soul.

The Vedic seers describe the material realm as consisting of three levels of worlds: upper heavenly worlds, lower hellish worlds, and the middle earthly worlds. Beyond this material realm exists the spiritual home of the soul, the abode of God. In its sojourn through the material world, the soul journeys through myriad planets, higher and lower, looking for happiness, looking for joy, looking for love. But the Vedas say that we can only find our true home when we give up our wanderings from hell to earth to heaven and understand the purpose of our soul.

The sages who have attained union with the Supreme Reality have revealed this wisdom: sentient beings are created for love. Even this material universe has been projected by wandering souls looking for love in all the wrong places. Material worlds exist so that we may fulfill the desires born of our free will and someday freely return to the spiritual realm. Only if we have free will, including the free will to make mistakes, can we ultimately reach the maturity to choose a relationship with God the beloved in the realm of the soul. So say the sages.

EINSTEIN'S QUESTION

Albert Einstein once said that the most important question anyone can ask is this: "Is the universe friendly?" By this Einstein was asking whether there is a higher plan in operation in the universe, which not only includes us but also has our best interests in mind. He declared his belief in a benevolent universe and famously remarked, "God does not play dice with the world." Is there a God? And is God favorable to us and our lives? The Vedic sages agree with Einstein. There is a God, represented in Vedic texts by the ancient word Om. One meaning of the word Om is "yes!" Yes: God exists, the universe is good, and all souls return to their Source in time.

In the Vedic understanding, there is no powerful devil fighting for supremacy over the universe. There may be demonic beings and there may be a supreme deceiver, but that being—like all beings—is subservient to God and Goodness. No being can challenge the supremacy of God or violate the universal laws. We can make free choices that lift us up to heavenly worlds and beyond or drop us back to remedial education in a lower world. As we sow, so do we reap. This is the universal law of karma.

KARMA AND REINCARNATION

Vedic wisdom informs us that karma is the principle of cause and effect in space and time in the lower, middle, and upper worlds of the material realm. Karma does not exist in the spiritual realm. We get reactions from the thoughts and actions that we take. Under man's law, a person may literally get away with murder. Under the universal law of karma, no one gets away with anything in the long run. Either in this life or in the next, our actions will return to us.

Our actions in this life determine our destiny in the next life. As a direct result of our karmic actions (good, bad, or mixed) during life on earth, we reincarnate in a new material body in an appropriate world. Predominantly good karma lifts us up to a heavenly world; bad karma lands us in a lower world; and mixed karma brings us back to an earthly existence.

We reincarnate in a physical body and a world appropriate to the desires and actions we cultivated in this lifetime.

Reincarnation is not simply a speculative Eastern belief. In recent years, reputable researchers such as Dr. Ian Stevenson of the University of Virginia and Dr. Brian Weiss of Mount Sinai Medical Center have documented hundreds of cases of people who remembered verifiable details of one or more previous lives.

Fortunately, we can transcend the laws of karma and reincarnation, even in this life. The spiritual path of bhakti yoga, India's way of enlightenment through love and devotion, teaches us how to act in such a way that no karmic reaction results. We act for the good of all by acting in devotion to God. These actions are transcendental and do not incur karma, which means that at the end of this lifetime there are no further karmic actions to be lived out in a material body in another material world.

WE ARE NOT BEING PUNISHED

According to the Vedic world view, we are not being punished on earth or after death by a judgmental or jealous god. The God of love allows us the free will to choose love or selfishness, heaven or hell. And as a prodigal son or daughter is always and at any time welcome to come home to a loving parent, so each of us will be welcomed home when we have learned the lessons of wisdom, kindness, compassion, and love.

It is to our great advantage to learn these lessons now, in this earthly school, rather than through an ongoing "school of hard knocks," birth after birth. Choosing wisdom now, choosing love now, accepting grace now is the intelligent choice for each of us. If it takes hitting rock bottom or a life-threatening illness in this lifetime to get us to this realization, so be it. In this sense, life's challenges, including serious illness, can be a blessing in disguise.

Preparing to depart this world in conscious awareness is an opportunity to let go of old karma, old patterns and addictions, and to embrace a karma-free life of devotion, which can propel us to the immortal realm of love. It is as simple as releasing old material attachments and attaching ourselves to the Divine.

THE SCHOOLS OF LEARNING

At present we are in the school of earth. A dull student may doze off in class and forget where he is. A rebellious student may waste his class time daydreaming or doing inconsequential things. Similarly, in the school of earth we have the free will to sleepwalk through life or to piddle our life away accumulating possessions, watching TV, and gossiping our way through the day. Yet we equally have the opportunity to grow in wisdom, compassion, and love.

We are immortal beings on an evolutionary spiritual journey through schools of learning in the material universe. Each lifetime, we enter a new classroom with new challenges and opportunities. Schooling means two things: completion of one grade and preparation for the next grade. We are here to complete the earth school lessons and to prepare for the higher schools to come and, ultimately, for graduation from all material schools.

Nearing death is like a wake-up call. It's like realizing there are only a few weeks until final exams. It is a time to catch up on missed assignments and review the entire semester. Knowing that we are nearing death is a blessing in one sense: We have time left to review our lives, bring things to completion, reconcile with others, and complete the inner lessons we may have missed. These final "school lessons" are often achieved with the help of a tutor—a spiritual master, or a friend advanced in spiritual matters.

SIGNIFICANCE OF THE
EARTH SCHOOL

What is the significance of this particular school of learning? The Vedas single out human life on the earth as a very special opportunity. According to the Vedas, there are 8,400,000 species of life on the earth. Human life is at the top of this spectrum, in the sense that we can understand that we are something beyond the body that we inhabit and are capable of reflecting upon our predicament. The Vedas also describe the opportunity to meet a realized spiritual teacher to help us in this school. Gaining a human form on earth and being guided by books of wisdom and a wise teacher enables us to finish up our schooling in this lifetime.

We have learned that there are three levels of schools in the material universe: lower schools, middle schools, and higher, heavenly schools. Pleasure in the higher planets is described as superior to that in other schools, but this can be highly distracting to the learner. And it is understood that the existential karmic pain of the lower planet schools is also very distracting. On the middle school of the earth, however, we experience the duality of both pleasure and pain. We see and feel both. Thus we can more easily gain insight into the temporary "ups and downs" that permeate the entire material realm.

THE MATERIAL UNIVERSE AS A PRISON SYSTEM

The Vedas have also compared the material planets to prisons of various degrees. We know that a hardened criminal may be sent to San Quentin, whereas a "white-collar offender" may do his time in a minimum security "country club" prison. Any prison, however horrible or nice, is still a place of restriction. The unlimited spirit soul is entangled in the material universe. This situation is painful, because by nature we are freedom-loving beings. We want to be in our home world, which revolves around love, freedom, and wisdom. But currently our choices continue to keep us in school or in prison.

The Vedas describe three levels of material consciousness: goodness, passion, and ignorance. Those people who fill their lives with ignorant choices—violence, laziness, cruelty, intoxication, and the like—will be transferred at death to an appropriate planet in the lower realms of the universe for rehabilitation.

Those who fill their lives primarily with passionate choices—obsessive work and money-making, excessive pleasure-seeking, and the like—will return to earth or an earthlike planet for another lifetime of remedial learning.

Those who fill their lives with good choices—acts of kindness, compassion, and morality—will go on to a minimum-security facility in a higher world.

We may wonder why the Vedas consider a higher, heavenly world analogous to a minimum-security prison. The Bhagavad Gita describes that all places in the material universe, including the heavenly realms, are temporary places of residence where old age, disease, and death are in effect. The soul is still not at home, even in a heavenly world, still not free from attachment and bondage, albeit a seemingly benign bondage. In truth, however, it is not benign, for the natural state and home of the spirit is full of unlimited happiness, wisdom, and eternality.

GOING HOME: ATTAINING THE SPIRITUAL UNIVERSE

How then can we graduate from all material schools or leave the prison system altogether? Let us look at this important question again. The answer hinges on the principles of free will and love. Existence, in the Vedic view, means the ongoing relationship of souls to the Supreme Soul—the relationship of all beings to God. Whatever else is going on is really only a background to this grand drama of love. Just as a person looking for true love may travel here and there experiencing happiness and distress, only when one's beloved is found does the greater life begin. The union of a soul with the soul's beloved is at the very core of the universal purpose. Life exists for love.

When we get tired of wandering the material planes looking for an unending happiness built on the ego and material unions, we become willing to sacrifice our self-centered will for the selfless will of divine love. *Yoga* means *union*. And the bhakti yoga of devotion leads us to an unbreakable union of love with God. The God of Vedic wisdom reciprocates that love in ways we cannot begin to imagine. This is the conclusion of the sages of India.

WAITING ON YOU ALL

"The Lord is awaiting on you all to awaken and see." So sang George Harrison, who was a serious practitioner of the Vedic wisdom. God not only awaits that sacred union with each of us, but actively participates in helping us along through divine grace, enlightened teachers, books of wisdom, our intuition, and myriad other ways. Included in the divine plan to support our journey back home are God's own incarnations on the earth at various times and places.

The Vedas teach that God comes as an avatar (one who descends from the spiritual realm) whenever the need arises in a particular world era. Avatars and prophets come to reestablish the path of religion by which each of us can ascend to our home to unite with God and our eternal sisters and brothers in a world not plagued by selfishness, old age, disease, and death. Krishna, Rama, Buddha, Christ, and others come at various times and places to reveal the message of detachment from the temporary and love of the Real.

As we awaken to the ultimate wisdom—that love of God, love of all beings, and love of our very soul is the goal of life—we are excited and inspired to "get on with it." We are motivated to drop the masks we wear, to let go of our obsession with possession, and to associate with like-minded spiritual people in order to obtain this union of love.

The nearing-death experience is a strong nudge to take care of business right here, right now. The human form of life on the earth planet is a powerful chance to graduate with honors, to finish up our wandering journey through the material universe. And what awaits us? Our true home, where "every word is a song and every gait is a dance." God and unlimited brothers and sisters from that spiritual realm are cheering us on.

It is the hour of truth for all of us. Our bodies are mortal, and death awaits each of us at a time we know not. In this very lifetime, we can finally wake up from the dream of bodily identification, birth, and rebirth. We can graduate from the material school of hard knocks and obtain our birthright of freedom, wisdom, and love. We can open our hearts to the mercy of God, join in the union of love, and go home. Our spiritual family awaits our arrival.

THE BOY WHO SPOKE WITH DEATH

Regarding souls and their destinations, there is an instructive story of a boy named Nachiketa narrated in the Katha Upanishad. As children, we often think more deeply, freely, and innocently than we do at any other time of our lives. We are not yet so conditioned by doctrines and prejudices. We may have the free time to gaze up at the stars, to daydream by a lake or ocean, to lie awake at night thinking on the mysteries of life, unbothered by the pressures of living and making a living. We may note that at the end of life this innocent, childlike state becomes available to some of us again.

Our teacher then on this journey is a child. The boy Nachiketa lived thousands of years ago in Vedic India. Nachiketa's father was of the priestly class (brahmins), whose duty was to give in charity for earthly benefit to others and for one's own personal benefit in the afterlife. The boy was concerned to see his father giving away old, worn-out cows in charity, rather than the man's prized possessions. Even a child could understand that the intent of giving was exemplified in giving one's best, not one's useless leftovers.

Nachiketa gently challenged his father about this. His father ignored the child. As many children will ask until they get an answer, Nachiketa continued to question his father. The boy finally said: "Why not give me in charity?" In guilt, irritation, and anger, the frustrated father yelled, "Yes, to hell with you!" By divine arrangement, the brahmin's curse was immediately carried out, and the boy found himself at the entryway to the abode of Yama, the god of death.

Being a bold and courageous lad, Nachiketa stood outside the doorway for three days, waiting to be received. When Death personified returned from a journey, he was greeted by a voice from the heavens chastising him for not properly receiving a guest, which is a sin in Vedic culture. To rectify his mistake, Yama offered three boons to his young guest.

THREE WISHES, THREE DESTINATIONS

Nachiketa's first wish was to be returned to his father on the earthly world and to be forgiven for his impudence. This wish was easily granted by Death. The boy's second wish was to learn the fire ceremony by which a person could attain a heavenly world after death. Yama not only granted this wish but said that he would honor the boy by renaming this ceremony the Nachiketa Fire Sacrifice. The boy now pondered his last wish. The child had often sat underneath the stars wondering about the stories he had heard of immortal life beyond the temporary earth and heavenly worlds sought by common people. "Is there a way to attain eternal life in a spiritual world, a way to become immortal?" he questioned Death.

Hearing this question, Death looked at the innocent boy incredulously. What did he say? Who was this child to have such thoughts? Yama's primary role as the judge of good and bad karma in assigning people to worlds appropriate to their actions in life was being challenged by this earth boy. What did he say? How dare he suggest a principle beyond the great law of karma!

I'll charm away this audacious question in no time, he thought. "Look, my son, take whatever boons you will. Beautiful dancing girls, the most chaste wife, a long life on earth and your next life in a heavenly world, earthly power and influence, thousands of first-class cows adorned with gold. All these things I can give you. Take them!"

Nachiketa did not pause to think but immediately replied, "And what is the use of all these temporary gifts if I am bound to death, rebirth, and death again in temporary worlds, life after life? No, my lord, I wish to know the great mystery of immortality. Tell me truly, is there an immortal world or not?"

DEATH, THE GREAT TEACHER

Now Death, the great teacher, smiled within his mind. Oh, this boy indeed is worthy to be my student. "Yes my child, sit while I speak to you of life, death, and immortality."

Yama told the boy of a Great Banyan Tree whose branches make up all of the phenomena and planets of this material universe, but whose roots are in the world of immortality, the spirit world of Brahman. "What is that world of Brahman?" the boy asked. Death spoke, "There shines not this sun nor moon nor stars. Neither lightning nor fire illuminates that immortal world. That world is lit by the Light of Spirit, which can never be extinguished. If one fails to realize God in this life before the bodily covering is dropped, he must again put on a body in another world of embodied beings."

Nachiketa was stunned and intrigued. He had never heard such things from his father or other priests, who seemed to do so many rituals for good crops, a good marriage, or at best, birth in a higher world in the next life. "And how, dear Teacher, may one gain this immortal world?"

"Ah," spoke the lord of death, "that is indeed a deep subject matter and a lifelong journey! Are you really prepared to follow this difficult path?" The boy nodded with a serious and determined gaze in his eyes. "Very well, listen carefully."

THE PATH OF YOGA

Death spoke of the human body as the City of Eleven Gates, referring to the eleven openings to the world of sense objects. He instructed how one can be the master of this city, instead of the slave of one's senses. Death spoke of the soul, hidden in the cave of the heart, which may be found through deep meditation. He spoke of the immortal path of yoga, by which one may break the shackles binding the heart to material desires and suffering. Yama further explained the yoga path in which individual effort, meditation, and the grace of God combine to lift one out of the world of samsara (death and rebirth).

Then the grave lord of death looked away from the boy, toward all living beings who would take birth in the earth world for millennia to come and said, "Arise! Wake up! Seek the guidance of a realized teacher and make your life successful. The spiritual way is a difficult but extremely important path. Do not hesitate to take it up in the human form of life!"

Nachiketa took the words of his teacher to heart. He rejected the ritual worship of his father and the priests of his time, by

which one could attain rebirth in a temporary heavenly world
at best. Nachiketa followed the path of yoga and gained the
immortal world of the soul at death.

AJAMILA IS SAVED FROM ENTERING THE LOWER PLANETS AFTER DEATH

In the story of Nachiketa, we discover the path by which one
either returns to earth, gains a heavenly world, or attains
the immortal spiritual world. The ancient scripture Srimad
Bhagavatam tells the story of Ajamila, whose bad karma actions
almost landed him in a hellish world at the time of his death.

In his younger years, Ajamila had been a pious man
belonging to the priestly class of Vedic society. He had exhibited
wonderful qualities of kindness, compassion, truthfulness, and
morality in his youth. Yet he became attached by sexual attraction
to a prostitute, eventually leaving his beautiful and loyal wife
to marry her. Ajamila spent the rest of his long life in sinful
activities: drinking to intoxication, lying, cheating, and taking
advantage of others to provide for his new wife and children. He
continued to produce children into his old age.

At the age of eighty-eight, he was very attached to his young
son named Narayana. The old man was nearing death. He could
actually see the frightening messengers of Death coming to take
his soul. In distress he cried out the name of his son Narayana
over and over again. Suddenly another group of beautiful beings
arrived, calling themselves the messengers of God. They stopped
the messengers of Death from taking Ajamila to the lower planets,
saying that he had resolved his bad karmas by unintentionally
calling out a name of God (Narayana) at the time of death.

This good fortune they attributed to the good karma gained
in Ajamila's pious youth. The messengers of God explained
to the messengers of Death that a powerful medicine, even if

taken without the knowledge of the sick person, can effect a cure. Similarly, one who is able to purify their consciousness at death through chanting the sacred names of God, goes beyond the worlds of birth and death. The messengers of Death left that place, knowing for the first time that there existed a power greater than death and karma.

LESSONS FROM THE STORIES OF NACHIKETA AND AJAMILA

In these two recorded histories from the Vedic wisdom teachings, the four destinations of souls are clearly described: hells, earths, and heavens in the material realm, and the immortal world of spirit beyond space and time. How to attain them is also explained. The wise young boy Nachiketa concluded that returning to the earth or even gaining a heavenly world was of limited value. His teacher confirmed that continuing to live in temporary worlds of karma was like a long, long night of dreaming. His teacher challenged him to wake up and follow the spiritual road to freedom and joy through the path of yoga.

Ajamila's sinful life was destined to take him to a fourth type of afterworld, a hellish planet where he would receive the actions of his present life. But he was saved from this karmic fate by chanting the karma-destroying Holy Names of God at death. In India even today many parents name their children with divine names to help all family members stay absorbed in sacred sound vibration as they call out to each other.

According to the Vedic sages, this ancient and approved practice of chanting the names of God is a method given as a special benediction for the age in which we live. Our very materialistic age, known as the age of Kali, makes living a karma-free life very difficult. As noted, God descends periodically to help us wake up to our spiritual life. God's name descends as well in this dark age to dissolve our unfinished karma and to open our heart to the life of the soul. The Vedic teachers encourage us to take up this chanting meditation at once. It brings joy to us in the present moment and prepares us for liberation at the moment of death.

Joyce was dying of throat cancer at the age of thirty-eight. When I met her she was sharp mentally but could not speak well because of the cancer. She was very skinny and pale. When Joyce showed me a picture of herself from a year ago, I was shocked. She was radiant and amazingly healthy-looking in her middle age. Joyce had come back to Christianity shortly after her diagnosis eight months ago. Her church had been helpful through visits and prayer, but she felt that something was missing. I asked if she had heard of the Jesus Prayer. She had not. I sat with her in her garage, and we chanted the divine names in this ancient Christian mantra for about fifteen minutes. At one point she jumped up and asked, "Did you feel that earthquake?" I had felt nothing. Joyce was very impressed with the prayer, which was punctuated for her by an inner earthquake. A few months later, she was at our hospice office facility, and I ran into her. She could no longer talk except in a whisper. Joyce was trying to tell me something, but I couldn't hear her. She put her lips up to my ears and whispered the Jesus Prayer. I was overjoyed that she was using this sacred mantra. Two days later, Joyce's husband called and said that she died in peace with the prayer on her lips.

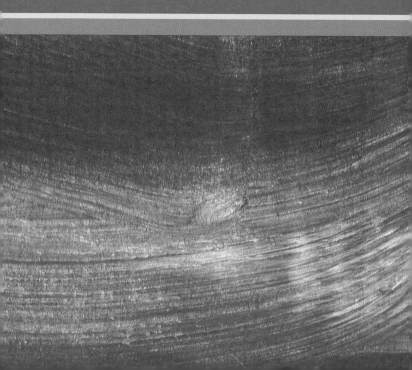

CHAPTER 4

CARING FOR THE SOUL

Caring for

the Soul

"One who sees the joys and sorrows of others as
if they were his own is the perfect yogi."
—Bhagavad Gita 6.32

A UNIVERSAL FAMILY

The concept of universal fraternity, "the world as one family,"
is one of the hallmarks of the Indian spiritual tradition.
It is not enough to strive for one's own enlightenment while
others suffer in pain or ignorance. As stated above, the true yogi
or spiritual aspirant feels the joy and suffering of others as his
own. Just as we walk the challenges of life with a beloved sister or
brother, we are encouraged by the Vedas to walk as family with all
human beings in their times of living and dying.

Today, many people in Western yoga communities greet
each other with the ancient Vedic greeting "Namaste!" Namaste

means, "I bow to the divinity within you." How can we see all living beings as one family? By understanding that the divine spirit or soul of each being is equal to all others. We may not be equal in intelligence, physical strength, or beauty, but we are all equal as spiritual sons and daughters of the Supreme Being. This understanding is at the heart of spiritual caregiving. Although a person may lose strength, mobility, and mental acuity as death nears, the spiritually attuned caregiver continues to see the dying person as the magnificent divine being who inhabits a now failing human body.

Accepting that we are a universal family, no one should die alone, uncared for and unattended. Whether we are biologically connected to a dying person or connected by friendship or by geographical proximity (perhaps to a dying neighbor with no family), we are encouraged to take up the role of caregiver if at all possible. Dying well is best done with support. And there will come a day when the roles are reversed, and we will need to be on the receiving end of this ultimate act of kindness.

LEARNING TO TRUST AGAIN

Caregiving has two aspects for a person facing death: self-care and care given by others. One way to care for ourselves if we are dying is by loving our self even as our physical body declines. Finding and maintaining our spiritual self-identity is one of the messages of the Vedic sages that we have explored in this book. Additionally, we facilitate our end-of-life care by trusting loved ones and friends enough to honestly face our own dependence, letting go of what we can no longer control and receiving the care others want to give us. We may fear slipping into dependence, feeling that we must stay strong and independent, take care of ourselves, and not be a burden to others. In most cases, however, there will come a time when this will no longer be possible.

As a child, we were dependent on our guardians. In time, by the natural laws of physical life, we may again become dependent on those who love us. Trust your friends and loved ones when they tell you that they want to care for you. At this critical time in life, the Vedas also encourage trust in guru, sadhu, and sastra: our teacher, other spiritual guides and friends, and the wisdom of holy scriptures. This trust and dependence is especially important as we seek to go from "death to immortality."

YOU ARE NOT A BURDEN

The greatest worry expressed by people who are dying is that they will become a burden to family and friends who will need to care for them. Caregiving is stressful for many people. However, for most caregivers, it is a sacrifice taken up as a "labor of love." When you find yourself entering the near-death stage, bless your loved ones or friends by allowing them the honor of taking up this labor of love. You will have completed the active part of your life. You will have given what you could to others; it will be time to receive from those who care. You are as worthy of care at this juncture in your life as you were as a child. Neither the dependence of childhood nor the end of life is unnatural or shameful.

If you are dying, trust your loved ones and friends who are stepping forward to help. The Serenity Prayer has helped millions of people to remember this important lesson:

Lord, grant me the serenity to accept
the things I cannot change,
The courage to change the things I can,
And the wisdom to know the difference.

Be wise. Let go of what you can no longer control. Let family and friends serve you and serve God by caring for you.

IF YOU ARE THE CAREGIVER

If you feel called to care for someone who is dying, be patient if they resist your initial offer to help. It is very difficult for anyone to accept the loss of their independence. Don't push your service on a dying loved one. Just be available and gently help them to become aware of what they can no longer do. Especially be sensitive to their wishes for caregiving. Let them maintain some control of their dying by following their wishes in the way you give care as much as possible.

But be aware as well that your ability to care for your loved one depends on taking care of yourself along the way—physically, emotionally, and spiritually. Take breaks as needed. Find family and friends to share the caregiving and to back you up when you need a rest. If you have a spiritual practice, it is a good time to reconnect to it. If you have a spiritual teacher, seek guidance. If you have books of wisdom that inspire you, read them again. It is a time of transition and challenge for you as well as your loved one. Reinforce your mind, body, and spirit with all available resources.

Roger had come home when he heard that his mother had an incurable cancer. Beth was only fifty-six years old. Her twenty-year-old son said that he felt resentful and angry that his mother was dying so early. But she had taken care of him as a child, and now he had come to take care of her.

Roger struggled with alcohol abuse and a very active, anxious mind. His mother had converted to Hinduism decades ago; her son was Jewish but was not practicing. Beth was advancing through the dying process very well. She was happy to be giving away her clothes, books, and spiritual items to special friends. She spent hours happily thinking of which gifts she would send to this friend or that family member. She continued her spiritual practice of scripture reading, meditation, and chanting sacred mantras. But as Beth declined physically over the next few months, her son became more and more depressed and anxious. One night he took an overdose of pain medication and almost died. Beth asked me to meet with her son at their home.

Roger said that the thought he could not get out of his mind was that his mother's life had been difficult, unsuccessful, and short. He loved her and believed that she deserved more than this. I brought Roger in to talk with his mother. With a serene smile, full of love and wisdom, Beth told her son that her life had been very successful and complete. She had made progress on her spiritual path and was ready to go on to a higher plane of learning. Her convincing words totally changed her son's attitude toward his mother's caregiving. Beth asked Roger to work with their neighbor Lori as a backup caregiver. She also advised her son to go to his faith and prayer for strength. Roger was able to calmly support his mother in the final days of her spiritual transition, once he understood and accepted her definition of a successful life—progress on one's spiritual path. At our last visit, Beth told me that Roger's peaceful presence at her bedside brought her the greatest comfort and joy, because it helped her remain calm and because she knew that he would be OK after she passed.

COMFORTING THE BODY, SOOTHING THE HEART

The Vedic tradition honors service to God and to others as the highest spiritual practice. Some caregivers are called to give physical support only. Others may give emotional or spiritual support. All forms of caregiving are significant and appreciated by a loved one who is dying. Often in a circle of family and friends, different people take up different tasks. This is not a time for competing egos struggling for the "best service." Work out a schedule of care for your loved one. Be willing to do any service that needs doing, including backing up a primary caregiver. There is always service to be done.

Sometimes private or professional caregivers are brought in to take care of some of the physical aspects of caring. A son or daughter may feel uncomfortable bathing their own mother

or father. This is normal. Make sure that your loved one is comfortable with the person who comes from the outside to do this type of service. There are, however, many physical support tasks, from feeding to changing bed sheets to giving medications, which most friends and family members can do. The operative caregiving principle at such a time is this: When no curative measures are possible, we can still comfort the body, soothe the heart, and care for the soul.

BEING PRESENT WHEN THERE IS NOTHING MORE "TO DO"

There will be other supporters who are best at just being with the dying person. You may be one of those potential spiritual caregivers. Especially in the West, much of our experience in giving care is framed in doing something for others. We wonder what we can do concretely for our friend or loved one. What tasks can we accomplish? Of course there are always tasks to be completed, but the dying person's life becomes simpler in many ways. He or she may spend many hours, days, and months bed-bound, unable to do much of anything. Does this mean the person has no other needs, that there is nothing for us to do? Not at all. In a recent Gallup poll, dying people were asked about their nonphysical needs. This is what they wanted:

Having someone with whom I can share my fears
    or concerns—55%
Having someone with me—54%
Having the opportunity to pray alone—50%
Having someone praying for me—50%
Having someone holding my hand—47%
Having someone help me become spiritually at
    peace—44%
Having someone praying with me—44%
Someone reading devotional materials—32%
Someone performing religious rituals—21%

Most of these needs may be seen as spiritual needs, not requiring us to "do a task." People nearing death are asking that someone sit with them, hold their hand, pray, and be a presence and a voice for spiritual peace. Some of us may feel uncomfortable not being able to "do something" for our loved one. That is fine. But if we are able to just be with our friend or family member, sometimes that is the best support we can give. In the list above, being trumps doing in terms of our loved one's needs nearing death. One conclusion we can draw from this list is that many people really want a calm, mindful person to be present for them amid the rapid changes, chaos, and confusion that may accompany the dying process.

A SPIRITUAL FRIEND FOR THE JOURNEY

The calm attendant a dying person needs may be a family member. Often, however, family members are unable to maintain a serene demeanor because their emotions are running wild as their loved one is slipping away. A spiritual friend may be the best person to be present for the dying man or woman on the last leg of their earthly journey.

Spiritual support may take many forms. We have seen that much of the support needed is gained simply by a spiritual friend being present in a compassionate, nonjudgmental way. That friend may sit silently, listen to his or her friend's concerns, pray or meditate with that friend, chant sacred hymns and mantras, read from inspiring scriptures, or create a sacred atmosphere with music and incense. Sometimes a dying person may ask to be taken to a temple or a holy village before they pass away. If this is impossible, the Vedic sages advise us to create a sacred place wherever the person is staying. Whatever helps the dying person to take shelter in their soul and in God will be the greatest support that can be rendered.

Remember that your dying friend will be leaving this world shortly and needs to raise his or her consciousness in order to attain a good destination. A spiritual friend can help the dying person focus on two things: letting go of any burdens or desires that would divert their journey from the highest goal, and reaching out to the grace that is abundant in the nearing-death time.

ACCESSING YOUR PEACEFUL PRESENCE

A true spiritual friend, whether family member or acquaintance, is on a journey along with the loved one who is dying. Being a calm and compassionate presence for our loved one requires us to be active in our own spiritual practice. The Vedic tradition counsels us to reach a deep and peaceful spiritual support state through the use of mantra meditation. If you do not have a meditative practice, you may try this simple method:

Choose a sacred word or phrase that honors your spirituality. If you do not find a sacred prayer that feels comfortable, you may use one of the Vedic mantras in appendix A.

Sitting quietly at the bedside of your loved one, breathe slowly and deeply while chanting your sacred mantra or prayer, either softly out loud or silently.

Fix your mind on the sacred mantra. As other thoughts arise in your mind, do not be disturbed. Let the arising thoughts float by like moving clouds while you calmly repeat your prayer.

If your loved one wishes to join you, that is wonderful. If not, simply continue the prayer and go deeper into the sacred presence, which will bring peace to you and your loved one.

WHAT WE CAN DO IF THE JOURNEYER IS UNCONSCIOUS

It is not unusual for people approaching death to sleep a lot, or even to enter an unconscious state. This does not mean, however, that they are altogether disconnected from the external environment. The Vedic literature tells us that hearing is the last sense to depart the dying soul. I know from my hospice experience that this is true. Several people who have come out of an unconscious state have told me that they were still able to hear what people in the room were saying to them or about them.

In the Vedic tradition, a spiritual friend or family member will chant mantras, sing devotional prayers, and read scripture in the dying person's room, even if he or she is unconscious. Traditionally, these words were spoken into the dying person's right ear. The scripture reading is often a passage about death and dying chanted in Sanskrit or English as guidance to the departing soul. Verses from the Bhagavad Gita are often chanted to the dying person:

Know that spirit that animates your body to be indestructible. Nothing can destroy you, the imperishable soul. Leaving your body, remember God alone, and you will attain the highest destination. That supreme destination is called unmanifested and infallible. Going there, you will never return to the material worlds.

If possible, a relative will put water from a sacred river like the Ganges and a leaf of the sacred Tulasi plant in the mouth of the dying person. These and other activities are considered purifying actions for the transitioning soul. The idea is that the departing souls should be as pure and free from karmic baggage as possible during their passing.

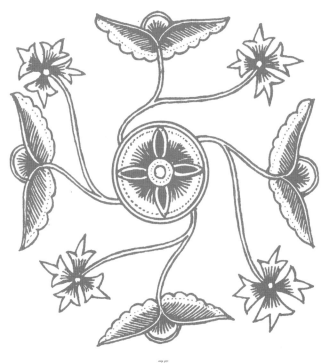

THE BENEFITS OF SPIRITUAL CAREGIVING: LEARNING TO DIE WELL SO THAT WE MAY LIVE WELL

In the Vedic tradition, our entire earthly life came to be seen as a pilgrimage through this temporary world to the immortal land of our soul, the spiritual world of infinite freedom and love. Caregiving for a soul nearing death means journeying with our dying friend or family member through the final stage of their earthly pilgrimage. Our sacrifice of love in joining our loved one's final journey has benefits to our life experience as well.

As we travel with a dying loved one through his or her last days, we clearly see the stages of detachment through which we will need to pass in our own life before being prepared to die. In other words, we learn to die well so that we can then live well, free from the fear of inevitable material losses. The Vedic aphorism to "die before you die" also addresses the wisdom of gradually dying to the ego and its trappings in order to fully live.

Death is so often seen as a tragic thief of life, a destroyer of dreams. This is no doubt true on the human side of life. But, on the spiritual side, we are inspired to see so many people in the nearing-death experience letting go of the finite things and bonds of this world, and literally reaching up toward a heavenly home world at death.

Life is a pilgrimage from birth to death. If we take insights from our journey with a near-death traveler, we will find our own life fuller and less worrisome. Especially if we can glimpse life through their eyes for just a moment, we can gain a whole new perspective on the preciousness of our own life. We can clearly see what is important and what is not—what is Real and what is unreal.

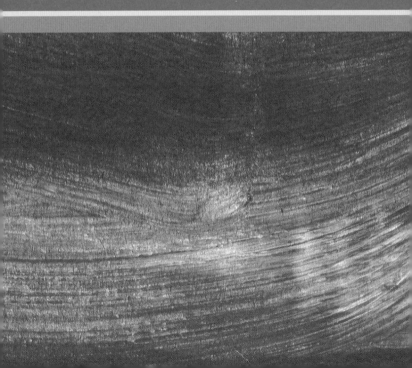

CHAPTER 5

GRIEVING AND THE END OF SORROW

Grieving and the

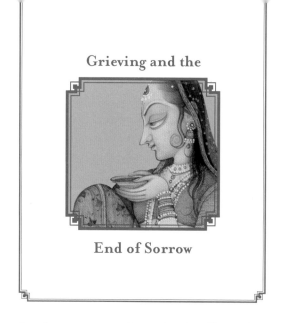

End of Sorrow

"Two birds, intimate friends, dwell on the same tree. One eats the sweet and bitter fruits of the tree; the other looks on in silence. The fruit-eating bird, who is the soul, sits plunged in grief. But turning to behold his joyful friend, the Supreme Soul, his sorrow is relieved."

—Mundaka Upanishad 3.1.1–2

HEART OF SORROW, HEART OF JOY

When a loved one dies, our heart cries out in loneliness, anger, or grief. We want to hide from the world or to strike out at it. We feel that our life will never be the same. Darkness and sorrow seem to have triumphed over goodness and light.

When a loved one dies, our human heart is pierced by the arrow of sorrow, which is feared but never expected. It happens to others, we think, but not to us. Questions swirl in our mind. Why did it happen to me? Did I do something wrong? How will I go on?

We know that the physical heart is the pump that sends blood to all parts of the body, sustaining life. But on the emotional level, the heart is the place of human feelings, of dualities such as joy and sorrow, anger and empathy. This heart is where the sorrow of loss is felt. To the human heart, the death of a loved one is perhaps life's greatest tragedy.

The Vedas speak of another heart, the spiritual heart, which is said to be the very home of the soul. *Hridaya* is the Sanskrit word for *heart* meaning "the seat of God." Accessing this divine heart is our hope for a lessening of sorrow and a return to joy as time passes.

The Upanishads speak of a "golden city of the heart where God dwells, indivisible and pure, the radiant source of all light." When we have suffered the ultimate loss of a loved one, the Vedas proclaim that only by receiving God's grace and love can our sorrow be relieved. This divine help may come through the agency of a family member or a spiritual friend, a counselor or minister. Sometimes help will come directly from a divine voice within the heart itself. The voice of the Supreme Soul speaks to comfort us in our loss. Then the heart becomes a source for regaining our joy.

TWO SWANS IN THE LAKE OF THE HEART

A story is told in the Vedic scriptures of a queen whose husband died deep in the forest. The king had given up his active life and retired with his wife for a time of spiritual practice. As he sat in his final meditation, the queen gradually noticed that his legs had become cold. Realizing that the king had died, she shouted out in great sorrow, begging him to return, and finally fell down at the feet of her dead husband crying pitifully. The queen then prepared a blazing fire to burn the body of the king. Shocked and inconsolable, she thought to commit suicide by entering the fire with her husband's body.

Just then, a gentle sage appeared in that solitary place and began to pacify the grieving queen with sweet words. "Don't you recognize me?" the sage said to the queen. "Can you not remember that in the past you had a very intimate friend? You may remember that you have consulted me in times of great need. My dear friend, both you and I are like two swans who live together in the lake of the same heart. Although we have lived together for many thousands of years, we are far away from our original home."

Earlier we explored the Vedic understanding of the three different aspects of God, including paramatma, the Supreme Soul within one's heart, which is the inner divinity. The mysterious sage told the queen that He, as the inner divinity, had always been with her throughout her many lifetimes, and that she would never be alone. She would always have an intimate friend from whom to seek counsel in times of grief and sorrow.

The Upanishads speak of the relation of our soul with the Supreme Soul in a beautiful metaphor: as two birds on the same tree of the body. One bird, our soul, eats of the sweet and sorrowful fruits of life. The other bird, the Supreme Soul, looks on, waiting for us to turn to God for guidance and help. In the great sorrow of a loved one's death, we can go deep into prayer or meditation and receive divine consolation from the presence of God within our heart.

A BRIDGE BETWEEN THE WORLDS

Walter loved his wife more than anything in the world. As fifty-three-year-old Bonnie slipped closer to death, Walter spent almost every waking minute at her side. The children worried about their father and what would happen to him when their mother died. Bonnie was a fiery, charismatic woman who loved life. Her impact on Walter and her children was strong and positive. I enjoyed my visits with Bonnie and Walter. Bonnie loved to joke around and laugh. She also enjoyed our talks on spirituality and God. Although she and Walter were Christians, they did not attend church regularly. As she declined, Bonnie asked me to come by more often and pray with the whole family.

When the hospice operator told me that Walter was on the phone, I hesitated before answering. I thought of how close Walter and I had become. He had revealed to me his doubts and fears about this life and the next. He worried about himself after his wife's passing and about his wife's destination after death. I was surprised to hear Walter say in a calm voice that Bonnie had passed in the night. He told of how she had seen a being of light in her room, and how he felt that she was walking between the worlds in her last two days of life. Walter asked me to meet the family at their home for a bedside prayer before his wife's body was taken for cremation.

When I arrived, he looked shaken, but he again told me of the unusual events surrounding his wife's passing that had given him comfort. As I held hands with the family and said a prayer beside Bonnie's body, Walter shed tears and kissed his wife goodbye for the last time.

As we stood outside the house, Walter told me that he now had a real experience of the spiritual realm. He knew that Bonnie would be in a better place and that he would be comforted by the spiritual realm. As he said "I now know that God is real," I looked into his eyes and saw a different man than the worried, anxious husband I had seen at my last home visit before Bonnie died. Walter's journey with his wife to the bridge between the worlds had given him the strength he would need during his grieving process.

HOW TO GO ON AFTER THE SHOCK OF DEATH

The Vedic queen was able to see and speak directly to her inner divinity after the shocking death of her husband.

Walter had a brush with the spiritual realm before his wife died, which helped him later in grieving. For most of us, grief will be lessened in a more normal way. After the death of a loved one, a grieving period is needed for most people as a time of healing the wounds that are caused by the arrow of sorrow. To ignore or minimize this need is unhealthy for one's body, mind, and spirit. Every person grieves in his or her own way and completes the grieving process in the survivor's own time.

Advice is plentiful as well-meaning friends struggle to bring a survivor back to a feeling of normalcy. But what grieving people want most of all is a compassionate person to listen as they attempt to process what has happened. What happened during the life of the deceased and the survivor? What happened to bring on the death of the deceased? What happened at the death of the deceased? What will happen to the survivor now?

These "what happened" questions give an indication of the most common initial response to a loved one's death: shock. Shock that my loved one is gone and will not return. Shock that death has so much power over my life. Shock that I was not prepared. And, significantly, shock that it could happen to me. Like an unexpected and unpredicted earthquake, death brutally awakens the senses to the fragility of human life.

THE STAGES OF GRIEF

Although no one person grieves like another, there are some common stages that the bereaved person may go through. If you are grieving or are called to help a grieving person, it is helpful to be aware of these stages.

Shock. We spoke of the shocking realization that our loved one is really dead and that we will die ourselves someday.

Searching. For some time after the death of a loved one, the survivor may turn to a person who is no longer there to make a comment or ask a question. He may pick up the phone expecting to hear the voice of his loved one. She may reach out in the night expecting to touch the body of her beloved. This is normal and is not usually a cause for alarm. Generally this searching and yearning for the deceased will end or greatly decrease in weeks or a few months. The human heart realizes what the mind already knows: my loved one is gone and will not return.

Despair. When the searching begins to come to an end, and we know that we will not see our loved one in physical form again, a period of despair may creep into our lives. This can be one of the most painful periods of the grieving process. This is a very important time for empathetic, listening friends to be available.

Regret/anger. Sometimes as one comes out of despair and depression, regret and anger take its place. Did it really have to happen? Was there something that could have prevented my loved one's death? Where was God when this happened? Again, a loving friend or counselor to listen, and a support group with other survivors, can contribute to a better transition through this period.

Reintegration into the world. At some point, most survivors see the possibility to reintegrate back into the world. By surviving the death of a loved one and the grieving rite of passage, the bereaved person often has developed enough inner confidence to take up the task of living again. Friends at this point can help by treating their friend or relative normally again. Also, letting the bereaved know that life will be different now, but not necessarily less than before, will be good counsel.

Survivors often want to understand the significance of their loved one's life and legacy, and whether the love that they had together will be finished with death. We have looked at the stages of grief due to losses associated with the death of a loved one. But what has not been lost? What can never be taken away from us? There are three important things about our loved one's life that remain with us:

> The memory of our loved one
> The legacy of our loved one
> The love we still share

I have heard many people nearing death say the same thing: "I want to know that someone will remember that I lived. I want to know that someone remembers what I did with my life. I want someone to know that I loved and was loved." Those who are left behind become witnesses to their loved one's life.

We have noted that sharing memories with good listeners, family, and friends is very healing. What is the role of legacy? Perhaps the greatest way in which we can honor a loved one's legacy is to choose to live out a good quality that they possessed. A father was kind, and we choose to live a kinder life. A wife was compassionate, and we choose to honor that quality in our life. A daughter was humorous, and we bring more humor into our life to honor her.

In this way, our loved one's legacy is not subject to the decay of material achievements but is transmitted on throughout the generations. They live on because we learn from their life some special quality which we then carry on in the world—in our own

lives and possibly in the lives of our children or friends who may emulate us.

Most importantly, we honor our departed loved ones by carrying in our hearts and in our actions the love that marked our relationship with them. It is a fact that love rules supreme. In our hearts, we know it. The special relationship we had with a loved one cannot be severed, even by the death of the physical body. We feel it sometimes. Deep inside we know that the powerful tie of affection—soul to soul—is still there. And at certain moments, we are certain that we feel a subtle tug on our heartstrings that feels so familiar. Thus we go on with our lives, honoring our departed loved one, honoring their life and legacy, and continuing to feel the love that cannot be diminished by time, space, or even death.

WHERE HAS OUR LOVED ONE GONE?

Grieving people often seek to understand what has happened to their loved one. Does he live on? Does she have a life somewhere beyond this world? Earlier, we explored the various destinations of souls. It is of the greatest comfort to know, according to Vedic teachings, that all souls are on a journey back to our common Source, back to God. And every soul's journey will end in the spiritual world. We will indeed meet our loved one again, perhaps in another world within space and time, and ultimately in the home of all souls beyond space and time.

Especially if a person has lived a good life, we can be assured that they will go to a higher, heavenly plane of existence for further evolution. And even if our loved one lived a life of bad deeds, we can know that he or she will continue their journey toward the Source as well, after they complete a time of remedial schooling. The bottom line is this: All souls are immortal and dearly loved by the Supreme immortal soul. We need not worry about the fate of our loved ones or their ultimate destination.

FINDING OUR SECURITY AGAIN

Looking over the entire grieving period, we notice that two big losses are being processed simultaneously: the loss of a loved one and the loss of the survivor's own sense of security. My loved one was mortal; I am mortal. He or she died; I will also die. The Indian sage Yudhisthira was once asked what he believed was the most amazing thing in the world. He immediately replied: "Although everyone knows that all people die, no one believes that they will die." This common human illusion of false security is shattered by the death of a loved one.

It is said in India that people who go through the death of a loved one experience a special form of spiritual awakening, smasana-vairagya: detachment at the graveside. I have seen this during many memorial services. For a brief moment, family members and friends become very philosophical while looking at the dead body or ashes of their loved one. They contemplate their own mortality. Unfortunately, this philosophical inquiry is often short-lived.

In fact, inner inquiry after the death of a loved one can be a very helpful part of the healing process. It has been wisely said that just as death is a rite of initiation for the dying person, so is that same death a rite of initiation for the loved one left behind. In order to heal, survivors will be challenged to create a new and more reflective life for themselves.

Why is this important? Before the death of a loved one, things seemed secure. Following the death, nothing may feel secure. Financial security may be threatened. Interpersonal security may feel threatened. And especially one's own physical security may feel threatened. The time for an innocent sense of false security is over. The survivor has an opportunity now to look for security in the spiritual realm.

THE JOY THAT ENDS ALL SORROW

Awakening to one's human mortality and divine immortality is a key realization that can lead to the end of grieving and sorrow. As humans, we rightly grieve the loss of a loved one in the depths of our emotional heart. This is healthy and helpful. We process what happened. We reflect on the deceased person's life, legacy, and love. Eventually, we reintegrate the experience of our relationship with our loved one and create a new life for ourselves.

Life will never be the same after such a loss. But the sorrow of that loss can end with the flowering of inquiry within our spiritual heart: Who am I? How has my life been changed by my loved one's death? How can I now live in a mortal world as an immortal being? The Vedic sages declare that the debilitating impact of life's unexpected sorrows can be alleviated through an understanding of our immortality.

The emotional roller-coaster ride of security and insecurity, joy and sorrow, and the like can be left behind when we embrace our true nature as immortal souls, beyond birth and death. Reconnecting to our spiritual practices, remaining open to God's grace, conversing with teachers and friends who are spiritually wise, and accepting the guidance of our inner divinity can help us find a resolution of suffering.

In life, joy follows sorrow, sorrow follows joy. The events of our lives remain in control of our on-and-off happiness until we find the deep, unshakeable happiness of the soul, ananda, the joy that never ends. It never ends—neither in this life nor in the next. So declare the sages of the Vedas.

If you are grieving, know that in time you will be able to listen to the comforting voice of your inner guidance as well as to trusted friends and advisors. Give yourself the time you need. Know this through your intuition rather than your mind or someone else's opinion. Your loved one is gone from this life. But, like the grieving queen who lost her husband, know that you have an eternal Friend who will continue to travel with you not only in this life but through the gates of death and beyond. And there are friends of this world to travel on this earthly journey as well.

If you have been called to comfort a bereaved person, work with the survivor's own inner spiritual guidance. What do they feel in their heart of hearts? Do they feel despair or comfort, fear or hope, anger or helplessness? Don't preach at the grieving person about God's love and care. Just listen to their concerns and realizations. In time, most survivors who access their innate spirituality will be able to hear the voice of a well-wishing friend as well as the voice of their inner divinity. Gradually, with the help of friends and of God, they will come to the end of sorrow.

In this book, we have made a short journey together through life and death, bereavement, and a return to the world. Knowing the immortal nature of all beings, children of the One Divine Being who is our Source, is the ultimate realization given by the Vedic sages to help us live a spiritual life of freedom in the material world. The Bhagavad Gita gives us a way to keep this understanding in our mind and heart:

> For one who sees Me everywhere
> and sees everything in Me,
> I am never lost to him,
> nor is he ever lost to Me.

Death is the greatest loss in our material reality. But the innate connection we have to our immortal soul, to other souls, and to the Supreme Soul is a reality that can never be lost. Understanding this truth is the joy that ends all sorrow.

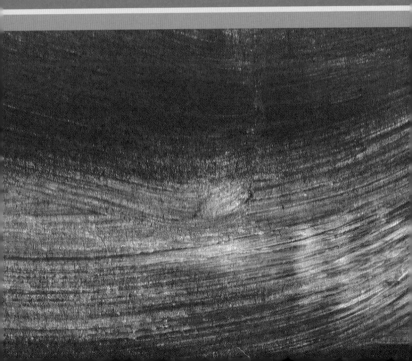

APPENDICES

APPENDIX A

Vedic Sanskrit Mantras

Sanskrit is said to be a divine language or "the language of heavenly beings." *Mantra* means "mind liberating." These mantra-prayers can bring one to a deep inner peace when chanted with attention and sincerity.

Om

Hari Om

Om Namo Bhagavate Vasudevaya

Sri Ram Jaya Ram Jaya Jaya Ram

Govindam Adi Purusham
Tam Aham Bhajami

Govinda Jaya Jaya Gopala Jaya Jaya

Radhe Shyam

Hare Krishna Hare Krishna
Krishna Krishna Hare Hare
Hare Rama Hare Rama
Rama Rama Hare Hare

What does the Vedic tradition say about life and death?

1 — All beings originate from One Source, the Supreme Being, who is both the Transcendent Supreme Person and the Underlying Reality of all phenomena, both material and spiritual.
Implication: Life originates from a Primal Source and reaches completion and maturity in a return to that Source.

2 — Each person is a beloved child of the Supreme Being and will ultimately return to union with that One Source. Not a single soul will fail to return to God in course of time.
Implication: No one suffers in an everlasting hell. A lifetime of bad deeds may result in a next life of suffering, but eventually all souls return to God.

3 — Each person is a soul, an eternal spirit, who inhabits a physical body during this earthly existence. That soul cannot be harmed or diminished in any way, regardless of what happens through the changes of the body.
Implication: We are spiritual beings inhabiting a physical body on a temporary journey in this material world. If we identify with our soul, suffering due to body-mind identification is greatly diminished.

4 — The inherent nature of each soul is *sat* (eternal), *cit* (full of wisdom), and *ananda* (joyful). Experiential discovery of the soul's nature is called self-realization.
Implication: Realizing our inherent true nature as eternal, wise, and joyful beings keeps us in a state of healthy self-esteem and strength, even in the midst of physical, mental, or emotional decline.

5 — Experiential discovery of our relationship to God is the ultimate goal of life and is called God-realization.

Implication: Discovering and cultivating our relationship to God keeps us open to receiving the grace of God as support through difficult and challenging times.

6 – Yoga, the Vedic spiritual path, culminates in self-realization and God-realization.

Implication: Following a spiritual path is important in order to realize our true nature and to be aware of the ongoing grace of God available to us.

7 – Karma is the law of cause and effect, in which every action taken has a resultant and appropriate reaction. These reactions to our choices create our destiny in the form of a new and appropriate embodiment after the soul leaves its current physical form at death. This transmigration (or reincarnation) of the soul into a new body is called rebirth.

Implication: Death, the end of our physical body, is not the end of us. Our actions and desires create the matrix for a new, appropriate physical embodiment through rebirth.

8 – A person can end the cycle of death and rebirth (and resolve all karmas) by his or her spiritual efforts and by the grace of God.

Implication: All karmas may be resolved and the cycle of physical embodiments may be ended through spiritual effort and God's grace. This is the goal of the spiritual path: to end the cycle of birth and death and to attain union with God.

9 – A person may practice detachment from the temporary world of matter and attachment to the permanent plane of spirit throughout the stages of life, thus living life fully but being prepared for death.

Implication: Living detached from matter and attached to Spirit during one's life prepares us for a good death at any time.

10 – The moment of death is very significant, like a final exam, for in that moment our cumulative thoughts (desires)

and life choices (actions) determine our consciousness at death. If a person is conscious of his or her eternal relationship with God at death, that person obtains liberation. Thus, a Vedic spiritual practitioner seeks to remember God at death, especially by remembering and chanting the sacred names of God.

Implication: The moment of death, our final exam, can be a great and powerful rite of passage. Especially important in making a successful transition is our awareness of our soul and the Supreme Soul.

BIBLIOGRAPHY

Byock, Ira. *Dying Well: The Prospect for Growth at the End of Life*. New York: Riverhead Books, 1997.

Easwaran, Eknath. *The Mantram Handbook*. Tomales, CA: Nilgiri Press, 1977.

Feifel, Herman, ed. *The Meaning of Death*. New York: McGraw-Hill Book Company, 1959.

Kubler-Ross, Elisabeth. *Death: The Final Stage of Growth*. Englewood Cliffs, NJ: Prentice-Hall, 1975.

Levine, Stephen. *A Year to Live*. New York: Bell Tower, 1997.

Maharaja, Bhaktivedanta Narayana. *The Essence of Bhagavad-Gita*. Mathura, India: Gaudiya Vedanta Publications, 2000.

Mascaro, Juan. *The Upanishads*. London: Penguin Books, 1965.

Prabhupada, Bhaktivedanta Swami. *Srimad Bhagavatam*. Los Angeles: The Bhaktivedanta Book Trust, 1972.

Singh, Kathleen. *The Grace in Dying*. San Francisco: Harper Collins Publishers, 1998.

Tripurari, Swami B.V. *The Bhagavad Gita*. San Rafael, CA: Mandala Publishing Group, 2001.

Zaehner, R.C. *Hindu Scriptures*. London: J.M. Dent & Sons, 1966.

Zir, A., and Braun, K.L. *The Complete Life*. Honolulu: University of Hawaii Center on Aging, 2002.

ACKNOWLEDGMENTS

I would like to express gratitude to my wife, Ana, whose insights contributed greatly to this book. Her courageous reflections on the in-between state of her near-death experience were also very helpful. I also thank Arjuna van der Kooij for his excellent suggestions and text editing. And I offer special gratitude to my hospice colleagues for sharing their compassionate realizations on death and dying.

ABOUT THE AUTHOR

J. Phillip Jones, MA, LMHC, is a psychotherapist who served as an interfaith hospice spiritual counselor in Hawaii for over thirteen years.

Previous to his hospice work, Phillip traveled the country as a Hindu monk for six years, meeting teachers and practitioners of many faiths to learn about their traditions and to host them at interfaith gatherings.

Phillip has encouraged, counseled, and guided over two thousand hospice patients of all faiths and beliefs, including those more spiritual than religious, on the art of dying and finding peace at the end of their lives.

He has trained over a thousand hospice staff and volunteers to understand the existential and spiritual issues that arise near the end of life, and he has served on the faculty of two National Hospice Conferences. Phillip is the author of an audio training CD entitled *The Yoga of Living and Dying*.

NOTES

NOTES

NOTES

MANDALA

An Imprint of MandalaEarth
PO Box 3088
San Rafael, CA 94912
www.MandalaEarth.com

Find us on Facebook: www.facebook.com/MandalaEarth
Follow us on Twitter: @MandalaEarth

Library of Congress Cataloging-in-Publication Data available.

ISBN: 978-1-68383-443-4

Publisher: Raoul Goff
Associate Publisher: Phillip Jones
Creative Director: Chrissy Kwasnik
Assistant Editor: Tessa Murphy
Senior Production Editor: Rachel Anderson
Production Manager: Sadie Crofts
Designer: Amy DeGrote

The content of this book is provided for informational purposes only
and is not intended to diagnose, treat, or cure any conditions without
the assistance of a trained practitioner. If you are experiencing any
medical condition, seek care from an appropriate licensed professional.

ROOTS of PEACE   REPLANTED PAPER

Mandala Publishing, in association with Roots of Peace, will plant
two trees for each tree used in the manufacturing of this book. Roots
of Peace is an internationally renowned humanitarian organization
dedicated to eradicating land mines worldwide and converting war-
torn lands into productive farms and wildlife habitats. Roots of Peace
will plant two million fruit and nut trees in Afghanistan and provide
farmers there with the skills and support necessary for sustainable
land use.

Manufactured in China by Insight Editions

10 9 8 7 6 5 4 3 2 1